HeAVEnly PaREntiNG

A 40-DAY ADVENTURE
TO LEARN DIVINE DELIGHT IN YOUR CHILDREN

BreNt G. GriFfin, LPC, LSATP

MORGAN JAMES PUBLISHING · NEW YORK

HeAVEnly ParEntiNG

A 40-DAY ADVENTURE
TO LEARN DIVINE DELIGHT IN YOUR CHILDREN

Brent G. Griffin, LPC, LSATP

Copyright ©2006 Brent G. Griffin

ISBN: 1-933596-46-5 (Paperback)

Published by:

MORGAN · JAMES
THE ENTREPRENEURIAL PUBLISHER™
www.morganjamespublishing.com

Morgan James Publishing, LLC
1225 Franklin Ave Ste 32
Garden City, NY 11530-1693
Toll Free 800-485-4943
www.MorganJamesPublishing.com

Cover/Interior Design by:
Rachel Campbell
rcampbell77@cox.net

Habitat for Humanity®
Peninsula
Building Partner

Unless otherwise indicated, Scripture quotations are from the New King James Version of the Bible, copyright 1979, 1980, 1982, 1984, 1988 by Thomas Nelson, Inc., Nashville Tennessee.

This book is dedicated to the my children and the loving memory of my grandfather, Jerome B. Griffin.

Thanks for everything, Granddaddy. I'll carry the torch from here.

Table of Contents

Introduction

Your picking up this book tells me several things about you. One, you love your children and you want what's best for them. Two, you love God and you want to be sure that you parent God's way. I applaud your commitment to your children and also your Heavenly Father.

The purpose of this book is to help you grow in your walk with the Lord and to help you understand how your relationship with Him can be understood through our walk with our children and vice versa.

It is my desire that this book enriches and edifies you, offering hope, confidence, and renewal in your parenting. At the same time, I hope to bring a smile to your face through humor as you remember yourself growing up and how God has blessed you. Walking with Christ is a developmental process and if you are relatively new to the Christian walk, you may read words or terms that are unclear to you. As you go through this journey over the next 40 days, let me encourage you to reach out to those at a local church to help you if there are concepts that are unfamiliar to you. The worst thing you can do is allow yourself to become discouraged and buy into the lie that you're not "Christian enough," or that you cannot get through the parenting learning process.

The devotionals each have a subtitle. You're welcome to jump around and seek out the subject matter that best fits your needs at that time.

I want to take a moment to encourage you to take the time to complete the interactive application questions after each devotion. Be sure to read each devotion deliberately and purposefully. Reflect on God's word and how the story fits you and your circumstances. Pray for the Holy Spirit to work through you as you read the daily devotions. This

11

will help you track your progress as God softens your heart to better understand your children through Him in addition to *your own* personal walk with the Lord.

God has made us uniquely His, and I am definitely unique. The humor in this book may not be for everyone. God speaks to me through metaphors and analogies in my life. I spent much of my life in a legalistic religious context rather than a freeing relationship with Him. This book is a testimony to the breakthroughs He has made in my life by allowing me to minister to the Body of Christ through my humor and talents.

May God continue to bless you in your desire to know Him more.

In service to Him,

Brent

Never Too Old to Return

Day one

Now that my son is almost a toddler, I've noticed my five-year-old

daughter wanting to play with me the same way as I do with him, namely wrestling or being rocked. She likes to go back in time and be babied like him. Don't we all do that? Assuming your parents were nurturing, don't you miss Mom's chicken soup or maybe a bell you rang from bed to let her know you needed some soup or maybe some more ginger ale? Perhaps you once had a parent hold a cold rag to your mouth when you hung over the toilet and now there is no one there to hold your hair back but you.

Although my kids *try* to go back to when they were younger with me, we actually *can* go back to God as children. Those children's songs we learned in Sunday school still apply to us. We never really stop being His kids after all. We just allow the world to define us. We grow up, dress grown up, use grown up words and go to grown up jobs to pay grown up bills, but underneath it all, we are just children – scared, unappreciated, craving-for-attention children. Some of us have lost that feeling of being nurtured. Some of us *never* had it. Some of us were taught to deny ourselves and to only think of others, lest we be considered selfish. God wants us to seek Him out, so that He can answer that bell, hold our hair, and fill our cup.

Have you forgotten that God is your Abba (Mark 14:36)? If you think I'm talking about the rock group, you need to research and study the different names for God! He is our Abba, our Daddy. Some denominations talk about having a healthy reverence for God and may think Abba is too mushy. NONSENSE! It is important to fear the Lord in a *healthy* reverence, but not so that it *prevents* intimacy in getting to know Him. I don't like my children calling me "Father"…sounds too formal. Just as God can see *our* hearts, so can I see my children's hearts and their respect for me when they call me Daddy.

Application Exercises

How have I honored God today as my Abba?

_____

_____

_____

_____

Have I allowed myself to approach the throne like a child as He has called me or do I present a "false self" to appear "grown up"?

_____

_____

_____

_____

Day two

My daughter likes to come up every day and say, "Wanna see how talls' I am?" and she likes to do everything herself. She knows she's not a grown-up, but she wants to be. I think we do the same thing. How often do we want to prove to God how grown up we are and how much we can do for ourselves?

I also know that when my daughter wants to show me something, she really wants me to affirm how beautiful she is. She's looking for validation. I am all too happy to oblige. To see how important we are in our children's eyes and hearts is indeed humbling. I find myself seeking God for the same approval. "See how I taught Sunday School, God?" "See how well I treated that person?" "Aren't you proud of me, God?" If you give *God* the glory, and it isn't of your own flesh, and you're not puffing up your chest as the Bible says knowledge does (1 Cor.8:1), then you're okay.

Too often we get into this spirit of legalism (creating for ourself a rigid list of religious behaviors to appear "spiritual") where we think we need to impress God. We need to do things to delight God *from* acceptance not *for* acceptance. In the Old Testament, people used to give burnt offerings (sacrificing animals) to get back into God's good graces. Thank Jesus for his life on the cross that we are saved by grace, and we don't have to draw and quarter a cow with a hatchet in the backyard to impress God!

17

Just like my daughter, we like to prove to God we can do things by ourselves. There's an old joke that goes like this: Know how to give God a really good belly laugh? Tell Him *your* plans.

Ever listen to your children discuss fanciful things that *they* are going to do that day? Sometimes, it is really "out there" stuff. We just kind of look at them and smile saying, "Oh, you are, are you?" God reacts the same way with us. We need to go to the Lord in prayer and petition, with thanksgiving, and make our requests known to the Lord (Phil.4:6), not just do something of our own will and *then* ask God to bless it.

Application Exercises

How do I find myself trying to impress God? Do I do good deeds to glorify His name or mine?

_____

_____

_____

_____

What actions of mine demonstrate that I may be trying to earn God's love? Do my actions support that God's love for me is based on His desire to love me and not based on my works?

_____

_____

_____

_____

How can I glorify His name through my talents, goals, and dreams?

_____

_____

_____

_____

Day three

God Delights in Us

Have you ever noticed how pleased we are with the little things our children do? We praise infants for every little thing such as burping, pooh-poohing, smiling, showing teeth, using a spoon, drinking from a cup, and writing a name. Every little behavior becomes a major accomplishment to us. So are our accomplishments to God.

Whether you plant a flower, sing a song, or politely kiss your spouse in the morning, little things honor God. We are *His* creations, made into *His* image to do good works (Ephesians 2:10). Just as we stand back in awe of our children as we point up at the stage at our dressed up snap bean or sunflower in an elementary school play, proudly shouting, "Yep, that's my boy (or girl)," so does God when we honor Him, treating others in a Christ-like fashion, or just being able to dress ourselves up in the morning. You know, He laughs and enjoys us a lot. Like we do when our little girls try to fix their own hair in the morning and it ends up all matted and disheveled.

Remember the time you woke up in the early morning, showered, got dressed, and only then realized it was 2am? Are you smiling at that memory? Yeah, God got a kick out of that one too. He loves us. He enjoys us. He says we are wonderfully made (Psalm 139:14).

Application Exercises

What are some of the daily things I do that God delights in?

_____

_____

_____

_____

How have I appreciated the little achievements of my children?

_____

_____

_____

_____

How do I demonstrate being realistic in my expectations of my children, extending grace and patience along the way?

_____

_____

_____

_____

Modeling Servitude

Day four

I remember an old joke about parents having kids just so they can get their lawns mowed and the trash taken out. While we can all laugh at the concept, the question remains: are they our children or little servants? Christ teaches *us* to be servants and nothing reminds me more of that than 3am feedings. We often think *we're* in charge when really it's our children. We are the servants. When they cry, we go. When they need changing, we change. When they are hungry, we feed. When they need cuddling, we cuddle. We aren't *really* servants of course, but if we have a servant's heart as Christ commands us to, it helps to strengthen and sustain us through those dark nights.

Often times we'll play with our kids and let them win, just to equalize the playing field a little to build confidence. We play dumb sometimes, and let them volunteer to do things we can really do ourselves so that we may promote healthy sharing and giving. They're not servants, but we want them to have a servant's heart. We work diligently to reward hard work and model a spirit of giving with exclamations such as, "Time to donate some toys, kids!" "Time for our annual canned food drive", and "Yes, I'll take three boxes of those delicious cookies!"

Do our children see us lead through our servanthood, giving to others, sacrificing of our time and talents to further the Kingdom?

21

Or, are we confined in a Christian bubble, just ministering to each other, preaching to the choir per se? Jesus served one time by washing the feet of Peter, the man who would betray Him three times! How humbling! The *Son of God* washing *feet*, and of a traitor, no less! Keep in mind this is before the times of spa treatments, manicures, and sterile, polished cleaning instruments!

Sometimes we refuse opportunities to serve because we feel it is beneath us. Maybe we rationalize that acts of service are for others and that's just not our spiritual gifting. Yet with all Jesus came here to do, He, the Lord of Lords, and King of Kings, the Savior, the Messiah, took the time to bathe callused, corn-encrusted, blistered, bunion-loaded, dirty feet!

Application Exercises

How do I demonstrate acts of servitude to my children?

_____

_____

_____

_____

How do I role model a servant's hearts to my children and others?

_____

_____

_____

_____

The Value of a Name

Day five

Even at my age, I still get a big kick out of seeing my name on mail. It's so exciting to get a package in the mail, isn't it? The wait. The excitement. It's exhilarating. Kids love it too. A person's name is the most important word in their lives. Grocery clerks will look up from a daze when you actually use their name. They look at you with a startled expression as if to wake up from a zombie-like state to say, "You know I'm a real person?"

Don't you love the name, "Daddy" or "Mommy"? Isn't it great to hear our children call us that? God is our Abba, our Daddy, and He likes hearing His name too. That's why worship is so essential to our relationship with Him. The best news is that after a long day of taking care of the kids, when we get tired of our children's endless questions and the bombardment of "Daddy? Daddy? DADDEEEEE!" God doesn't feel that way towards *us*! He *likes* to hear from us. He *never* gets annoyed when we call His name. He *seeks* relationship from us. He created us for that fellowship *with* Him. From the fall in the Garden, man's sin interrupted our intimacy with God and it is only through a relationship with Christ that rebuilds that connection to God.

Application Exercises

How do I call upon the Lord in my daily life?

_____

_____

_____

_____

How might I worship God in a more intimate way?

_____

_____

_____

_____

Presence vs. Presents

Day Six

I remember the Dick Van Dyke show a lot growing up. He had a son named Richie. You didn't see him much and the biggest thing I remember about him is he always being at the front door when the father came home asking, "So, what did you bring me, Dad?" At which, the father would look in his pocket, hand him a piece of gum or a paperclip or whatever he had and then, depending on if it was legit or not, Richie would say, "Thank you, Daddy." The joke was you never knew if it was going to be a funny, "This stinks Daddy" thank you or a genuine show of gratitude.

However, one thing Richie never said was, "It's good to *see* you, Dad. I'm glad you're home." Often times we have a habit of looking at God as a cosmic genie. "So what did you bring me, God?" We sometimes overvalue blessings more than obedience, or honor and love. Just as we'd be disappointed if our kids neglected us as loving parents, and only saw us as present givers, God wants us to seek His face, not just His hand. While God is a loving Heavenly Father, and He does love to bless us, He also wants us to realize that the blessing is in the *relationship* not in the handout. Seek His presence, not His presents.

Application Exercises

How do I express gratitude for God? How do I seek His presence more than His presents?

_____

_____

_____

_____

What are the personality traits of God that I love? What are the qualities of our relationship that I adore?

_____

_____

_____

_____

Children love to climb. It's a necessary

stage of infant development. It's cute to watch them try and take risks. They're too young to know limits. I try regularly to raise my children like little daredevils because I want to instill in them a confidence that they aren't limited. The world will soon enough try to put them in a "box" defined by gender, socioeconomic class, attractiveness, etc. I also want them to develop a sense of resilience.

You can see a lot of different parenting styles on the playground. First, there are the parents who are over their children like hawks, quick to pick them up and guide them in the right direction. They mean well, but they are overprotective - teaching their children to fear the world around them. Second, there are parents who don't look or supervise their children at *all*. They just let them run wild - never paying attention to whether or not the child is in danger or endangering others. Third, there are the parents that give them enough space and are careful to watch, but *let their kids tell them* if they need them.

Have you ever noticed that children will look up at you when they fall to judge how bad it is? They look to us first to determine how serious an injury is. That's why I'm careful not to judge a fall a crisis before *they* do. Allowing a child to determine if they need help and to discern if a problem exists is part of healthy emotional management.

Doing this gives them a sense of empowerment, of free will, *but* with protective boundaries. Of course, when they *do* need help, and when they *do* cry on their own, it's important to always be ready as loving parents to kiss the boo-boos and hug them.

God does the same thing. He trusts us to depend on Him. He doesn't get us out of trouble right away. Sometimes we must learn to deal with the natural consequences of our actions. He just loves us *through* the pain.

Growing in the Lord and climbing in life to new heights, new ministering, and new witnessing takes tremendous strength, courage, and endurance, all of which cannot be done via our own strength, but through Christ's.

Application Exercises

How am I climbing and striving in my relationship with God and His will for my life?

_____

_____

_____

_____

How am I at extending enough free will to my children without being overbearing and yet still loving them, encouraging them that they're not alone in their battles?

_____

_____

_____

_____

Day eight

Bullying has become a real problem in our

schools. Our children may be picked on for being different, whether it is their skin color, religion, clothing, etc. Schoolyards are filled with bullies that try to feel better by tearing others down; offering dares and double dares to children with low self-esteem. These children are vulnerable to the tempting challenge to rise to a new status by ingesting a worm or calling a teacher a bad name.

Of course, the children aren't alone. This behavior can also be seen in the business world with corporate business people competing for salaries and promotions with dog-eat-dog tactics. The world pushes us forward to step on others on the way to the top. These tactics aren't original of course. The same behavior was seen in the desert by Satan tempting Jesus with similar dares: "If you're so great, why don't you turn that rock into some bread?" (see Matthew 4:1-11)

How often do we entertain those same notions? "If you're such a good parent, why isn't your kid making A's?" "If your child is so great, why isn't he the quarterback or she a cheerleader?" The church is not immune either. "If you're such a great Christian, why can't you read the Bible in a year or be on this committee or that committee?" All of this taunting - Dad not making enough money, Mom not having the house clean enough - and so it goes. Our children go through the same thing and need to know that they're special in our eyes. Not for

29

what they can *do*, but because they are *ours*. We can demonstrate this by modeling humility and not getting caught up with the Joneses.

That's how God sees us. We are significant not for what *we do* but for who we *are* in Christ and what He *already did* for us. We are God's children (1 John 3:1). He gave His only Son to die for us so that we wouldn't have to, but that we would have ever-lasting life (John 3:16). It's a gift. We just have to receive it. Too often we reject it, thinking there's a catch. We can't be happy with just Christ's fulfillment. We have to get our flesh tickled all the time with the latest gadgets, hobbies, toys, competitions, etc. All of this while Satan looks on, smiling.

Application Exercises

How does my lifestyle demonstrate that I am significant by who I am in Christ and not in what I do or what I have?

_____

_____

_____

_____

By what standard do my children base their significance? Where do they learn that?

_____

_____

_____

_____

Where's Your Treasure?

Day nine

My children are learning about money. They have a hard time knowing where it comes from. Remember Mom or Dad saying, "Money doesn't grow on trees, you know"? That's true, but today's kids think there is a magic treasure machine that we can visit called an ATM and at anytime, money is just free. It makes sense (no pun intended). We need money and they see us pick it up. They don't see the sweat and hours that go into our work behind the money necessarily.

The Bible speaks about our treasure being where our money is spent. What's *your* treasure? A lot of times we see our children wanting to spend money on *seemingly* frivolous things: a new dolly, a race car, or a piece of candy. Then *we* turn around and go get our double latte with extra cool whip and sprinkles, or a new magazine to find out who's dating who in Hollywood. We all have our little treasures. And there is nothing wrong with that. There really is nothing biblically wrong with having money. The problem is when money has *us*.

Part of the importance of teaching children the value of money is not just the balance between saving and spending, but also in *how* you spend and what you save *for*. Tithing is an important part of stewardship. Too often we give God chump change or whatever is left at the end of the month when the reality is, that everything we have, I mean *everything*, is His *anyway*. He *loans* it to us. Even when we

31

tithe, we have a responsibility to God in how we spend the rest of our money. One easy mistake to make is believing that financial blessings from God are to be used on *ourselves*. While we are never to feel guilty for being blessed, it is important to discern if that money is to be used to help a ministry, support a mission trip, etc.

Children learn about saving and spending from us. I remember a sign in my dormitory in college that said, "The world was not given to us by our parents, but loaned to us by our children." Hopefully, we're doing better in our lives sowing seeds and tending our "garden" than Adam and Eve did.

Application Exercises

Since the world is loaned to me, how do I make sure His will "shall be done on earth as it is in Heaven"?(Matthew 6:10)

_____

_____

_____

_____

How do I model good stewardship to my children?

_____

_____

_____

_____

God's Mentors

Day ten

Losing a parent is painful. Whether it's to death or just moving away for college or marriage, our relationships change and we're not as close as when we lived under the same roof. God has always placed parental-like figures in my life at each crucial stage of development. Perhaps you've noticed that, too. That older woman in the apartment across the way reminds you of your grandmother. The advice from a Sunday school teacher reminds you of something your father or mother would say. As the old slogan goes, "When the student is ready, the teacher will appear." God is ready to appear in our lives when we turn to Him for help. It is through the Body of Christ, the people of the church and the community, that He can minister to us.

I'm often reminded of the realization of other teachers in our lives every morning when I see my children off to school on the bus. I sometimes still have knots in my stomach as I have to turn them over to the world, trusting that they are in God's hands, and they will have other teachers, other mentors in their lives besides me.

I remember hearing the idea that faith is like reading Hebrew backwards. You have to look back over your life and see how God's faithfulness has been proven in the past to help sustain you in the challenges today and ahead. It is His faithfulness through my previous teachers that gives me confidence that my children will have other teachers to guide them as well.

Application Exercises

How has God's faithfulness been demonstrated in my life?

_____

_____

_____

_____

How do I practice turning my faith over to God with my children's care?

_____

_____

_____

_____

Day eleven

How many of us grew older and vowed not to become like our parents, only to say a "mommyism", or something "daddyish" when we got mad at our children? Yeah, it seems inevitable that our looks, style, laugh, and other idiosyncrasies of our parents come out. If we don't notice it, or we try hard to stifle it, our spouses are all too happy to point out to us how we're just like our parents!

Unfortunately, we may also deny how we have grown into the image of our Heavenly Father. Perhaps when we got saved we were fired up for God, and over time the bright light became a flicker. Maybe our friends noticed, and they said we're too "Christianny" for them and we felt embarrassed. It is difficult in this day and age to persevere in our sanctification and growing more like Christ in the face of a dynamic, secular world that values competition, biting humor, sexually explicit images, and tolerance for all views – even those that fly right in the face of God. The Bible instructs us not to keep our candle under a bushel (Mark 4:21). We need to watch out for the media and friends who walk around with bushels to snuff out our flame for Christ. He instructs us to be the Light of the World (John 8:12), with Him radiating through us.

Application Exercises

How do I demonstrate the brightness of His Light in Me in the midst of societal pressures to conform to a worldly norm and/or to compromise my Christian convictions?

_____

_____

_____

_____

What are the influences in my life that attempt to snuff out my flame?

_____

_____

_____

_____

Day twelve

A couple of years ago, the big fashion trend was the WWJD bracelets asking us to consider, "What would Jesus do?" Sometimes we as adult children may have asked ourselves what our parents would do. Then, as parents, we pray that all of our speeches and lectures will break through our children's defiance, so maybe they'll hear our voice and know what we would have them do when they face the challenges of life on their own.

The Bible says train up a child in the way he should go, and when he is old he will not turn from it (Prov.22:6). It is true that children do what we do and not what we say. In a daily walk with us, as they see us practice biblical principles and standards for life, they learn to model after us. The same is true with our walk and the Bible. It is only through a daily devotional time in God's word through which the Holy Spirit may be able to quicken us to a scripture that we read to help us in time of need. Just as we cannot afford to stray from biblical parenting so as to confuse our children, we cannot afford to stray from God's living word. Likewise, as we pray our words are in our children's head to look both ways before crossing the street, we need to make sure His word is in our minds and hearts so that we don't get run over when we cross those treacherous roads in life.

Application Exercises

Do I read and memorize the Bible enough so that the Holy Spirit
can quicken to me, through scripture, truth when I need it?

_____

_____

_____

_____

How have I role modeled to my children how to handle adversity
in life?

_____

_____

_____

_____

Grace in the Midst of Anger

Day thirteen

I never really understood the concept of separating the sin from the sinner until I had children. Whenever I would get mad at a person, how could I *love* them and yet hate what they *did*? It seemed to go hand in hand. I didn't like what they did, so I didn't like them. And yet every night when I tuck my children in for bed, no matter what happens during the day, and no matter how many times they disobey or stray, I love them. I love them for who they *are*, not what they did. Watching them sleep, they appear so innocent and I am reminded how God's grace is sufficient for the day. **Indeed**. So should our love for our children.

Just as the Bible says don't let the sun go down on your anger (Eph. 4:26), be sure not to carry a burdened, bitter heart towards your children into the next day. Go to God and ask for Him to restore you. Pray for strength and resilience to weather the storms of parenting and discipline.

When my kids screw up, my wife and I will regularly tell them how we love them but we don't like what they did. That's crucial because kids sometimes experience our anger as rejection, when the truth is we are protective. We don't want them to get hurt, and we want them to learn from their experiences. Unfortunately, children are like emotional sponges and cannot discern between their actions and identity when they absorb our feedback. They may experience rejection regardless of our delivery.

The same is true with God in that He doesn't want us to experience rejection. He loves us for who we are and not through our circumstances. I regularly hear in my counseling practice how a person thinks God is condemning them, and is unloving because of the circumstances they're going through.

While it is true that the wages of sin is death (Rom. 6:23), both spiritually and physically, and He *does* call us into a life of righteousness and will let us know when we stray, NEVER does He stop loving us. It is not in His nature. God *is* love. Just as it is written, nothing can separate you from the love of God (Rom. 8:38-39). While our children's behaviors may strain a relationship, just like our sin may strain our relationship with God, He still loves us. In the same way, nothing my children can do will stop me from being their father. In our homes we need to be sure that our love for our children transcends the circumstances, just like God's love does when we sin.

Application Exercises

Do I withdraw love and affection when my children disobey or do I love them through it while still being firm with consequences?

_____

_____

_____

_____

Do I harbor resentments towards my children from day to day or do I confess my anger before God and conscientiously decide to extend grace to my children the way He does to me for my sinfulness?

_____

_____

_____

_____

God is Too Much

Day fourteen

Have you ever noticed how kids love for you to share with them anything that you are eating or drinking? At night you would think that they become cacti because they *just have* to have that final drink of water. "*Please,* Daddy! Get me some water!" they cry out, parched with a dying thirst. As loving parents we oblige, and we reach out to them with this big glass of water, only for them to take a sip big enough to drown a *gnat!* They look up, smile and say, "Aahh. Thanks." That's it? We took this big glass of water to them so they can take a *sip*? Yep, and it keeps happening. "I'm thirsty. I want a soda" and then they only take a swallow or a quick gulp.

Ironically enough, while we strain to understand the logic of it, we as Christians do the same with our Heavenly Father. Spiritually we come dry to God and say, "Fill my cup," (see John 4:10) and it doesn't take much for us to enter into His presence or for Him to confirm His presence with us. The truth is, just as our children can't handle large amounts of water, we can't *handle* large quantities of God's holiness.

Sometimes I can discern my daughter's request for water, not as a sign of thirst for water but for *relationship.* If I come home late from work and I grab dinner while she gets ready for bed, guess who else is hungry? My daughter could be stuffed to the gills but she'll say she's hungry just to spend time with me and know that I'm there for her. Just like my daughter's stomach can't possibly hold the amount of water I brought, we cannot handle the true presence of God with our fleshly bodies. It would disintegrate.

Ever see on the news during hurricane season when the goofy weatherman shows how brave he is by standing in front of a huge fan to recreate the wind velocity he'd experience would it have been a true hurricane? His hair is flying, his face is pushed to the side like a face-lift on *Extreme Makeover*, and he can barely keep his stance. Imagine that multiplied by 1000 and that doesn't come close to God's magnificent power!

Application Exercises

In what ways do I need to have God fill my cup?

_____

_____

_____

_____

In what ways is God more than enough in my life?

_____

_____

_____

_____

In what ways do my children make requests for practical needs, when they are really communicating the need for relationship?

_____

_____

_____

Prayer Styles

Day fifteen

My son is crawling fast now, and he'll get up on his knees and hold his hands up for me to pick him up. When I stand right over him when he does this, he'll look way up and sometimes lose his balance and fall backwards. It really is adorable. At night in his crib, he'll lay on his stomach with his knees tucked in under him and his arms outstretched above his head. It looks terribly uncomfortable, and yet he appears peaceful. It looks like he's in worship.

Then again, his posturing always appears to be in worship because when you think about a baby's development, at birth they first lay down on their back or side, then they lay down on their stomach, then they get on their knees, then they stand. That's the exact order of our worship behaviors sometimes! Maybe at first we're in bed laying on our backs saying, "I don't want to get up and pray, God". Then maybe we get up, and if we're desperate, we lay on our stomachs with our faces to the floor. Perhaps, we get up on our knees, falling prostrate and looking up at Him with our arms in the air. If you really want to get into it, you stand up with your arms over your head looking up, praising, swaying, and worshipping Him with everything you've got!

There are many different ways to worship and many different stances based on personal preference and even denominational differences. If your heart is open and you're singing to the Lord, all of those worship styles are acceptable in His eyes.

Application Exercises

Which praying and/or worshipping positions most make me comfortable and feel connected with God?

_____

_____

_____

_____

Does my worship style reflect a personal relationship with Christ, or is it based on whatever my fellow church members do?

_____

_____

_____

_____

As my relationship with Christ grows, does my worship style? How?

_____

_____

_____

_____

Day sixteen

One day my daughter was in one of her rebellious moods and she was instructed to go to her room. Later, when I went in to visit with her, I sat on her bed while she was in the corner refusing to look at me, much less talk. I was not angry, and I felt much compassion. My body language and voice tone demonstrated this but she was not budging. She knew what she had done was wrong and I simply wanted her to apologize. Then we could kiss and make up. Being the strong-willed child that she is, she was having none of that.

I was so puzzled, and it reminded me of God and *our* unwillingness to repent, despite feeling convicted. I remember wondering how my daughter could reject me so easily. Didn't she *know* how much I loved her? Haven't I role modeled grace and forgiveness to her enough to know that I *mean* it when I say that we will kiss and make up after the apology? Was she *that* untrusting?

It was then that I realized we do the same thing with God. No matter how faithful He has been in the past, and no matter how much scriptural truth we know about God's love and His unconditional acceptance and forgiveness, we turn from Him as we get stirred up in our woundedness. We want to come to Him on *our* terms. That's what my daughter wanted to do. She wanted to be able to save face *and* still apologize. It wasn't about me anymore than it is about God in our life. It's about our sinful nature and our inborn desire to live independently from God.

When we feel convicted, we either move *toward* God or *away* from Him. My daughter had lost the knowledge of my overwhelming love for her and she could only concentrate on her willful defiance and shamefulness. I couldn't make her come back to me. I could only model understanding, compassion, and grace. It wasn't long though before she came back to my loving arms.

That's one of the hardest parts of parenthood: letting go and letting our children return to us rather than forcing them to prematurely, before the lesson is learned. Our children don't need to feel ashamed, but they do need to feel convicted enough that they seek us out for resolution. If we rush this process to justify our need to be accepted by our children, we've done them a great disservice. Having to *allow* our children to wrestle with the emotional consequences of their sin is difficult.

It *is* appropriate to check in with them from time to time. That does not mean we are to rescue them from the emotional task of reconciliation. Like God, we can love and accept them through their pain, but not necessarily take it away. The same is true with us and God's grace and mercy. He doesn't promise us a life without pain. He promises to love us through it and be with us as our Comforter. As we yoke ourselves to Him, He gives us the supernatural strength necessary to deal with the painful, natural circumstances.

Application Exercises

How do I model compassion and grace to my children?

_____

_____

_____

_____

How does my relationship and loyalty to God demonstrate the relationship my children have with me?

_____

_____

_____

_____

How was grace and reconciliation after conflict demonstrated to me growing up?

_____

_____

_____

_____

How do I cope with watching my children feel bad? Can I honor their feelings and love them through it, without feeling the need to rescue them or take their pain away? Do I look to God to strengthen me in ministering to them instead of relying on myself?

_____

_____

_____

_____

Day seventeen

Kids have so much energy. They help us stay in shape whether we want to or not. As we get older, we wish we could bottle up what they have and *sell* it. They get so excited at life, with such a renewed zest after achievements. At the same time, sometimes as parents, we expect too much of them or expect them to have as much endurance as we have. We can stay up longer, and our stride is longer, and occasionally they have trouble keeping up. Sometimes, we even think they should have the same amount of energy *all* the time. I mean, they are kids, right? However, this is not the case for them and neither is it with us in our Christian walk.

When we first confessed our sins to God and asked Him to come into our hearts, declaring Him Lord and Savior of our life, we may have experienced a new zest for life, a new commitment. Our emotions may have been flowing heavily, or we may have thought we just couldn't get enough of Jesus.

That soon began to wane though, as it does for all of us. Our commitment to God must be based on just that - commitment, not mushy sentiment. Just like in a marriage, commitment and friendship are needed to sustain relationship when the "love feelings" wane. It's great to have those mountaintop experiences with God, but if we are to truly conform to the image of the cross and grow. We must learn how to live in the valleys as well.

Anyone can be a great witness when they're on the mountaintop. The true testimony comes with how you live your life in the valley. And people are looking. We all experience trials and tribulations. It's just that, as Christians, we respond differently. If you look in the biography of any role model, you will find multiple failures and a resilience to get back up and try again.

Our lives are to be used as a message. People need to see how we manage negative emotions during crises. It's not about being perfect or hiding from our emotions, so that we look like proud robots. Emotions are God-given. We need to show people that they can manage and express emotions, and *still* make wise decisions in the midst of trials, relying on God for strength.

While my children have trouble keeping up with me sometimes, and also me with them, I'm reminded of how God never forsakes us when we're less faithful in our spiritual disciplines.

Application Exercises

Have I measured the maturity of my walk with Christ in terms of emotions or commitment?

_____

_____

_____

_____

Have I been unrealistic in my striving for emotional highs and looked at that as a measure of a "true" Christian? Why or why not?

_____

_____

_____

_____

What have friends, family, neighbors, and even strangers noticed about my Christian character during my personal valleys?

_____

_____

_____

_____

Day eighteen

My daughter and I walk to the bus together. Sometimes we skip, and other times we sing songs. I know how important it is for her that I get on her level. At the same time, there is that nagging part of me that is tempted to look around and see if neighbors are noticing me "acting the fool." Then, I'm reminded that the only person I care about right then is my daughter and how she looks up at me. It is in that instant, in my ability to fully be with her in a child-like fashion, that validates who she is as a person. The same is true in our worship with God.

I often have to close my eyes during worship at church, not because I want to look more spiritual, but because I want to block out everyone around me. Doing so helps me lock in on that God-me moment. I put my hands up and praise Him. This way of praise could open me up for ridicule from the congregation because the service I attend is rather conservative and only a handful of people do this. However, if I'm going to be a fool, I'm going to be a fool for Jesus. I don't mind being a fool for my kids either. They love it and so does Jesus. In fact, He laughs and sings with us on the way to the bus.

I remember clearly when I became free to worship God with confidence. I was at an outdoor rock concert - everyone was singing, dancing, and raising their hands. The Holy Spirit quickened me to how easy it is for us to celebrate and raise our hands for cultural icons at a rock concert and yet not the risen Christ at church?! Our priorities have gotten skewed. Who is *truly* worthy to be praised? I couldn't possibly offer more dramatic praise to a worldly band than God, who gives me life *eternal* and sent His Son to die for me!

Application Exercises

Do I worship God in service like it's a personal concert between He and I, or do I worship how everyone else is doing it?

_____

_____

_____

_____

How does my need for acceptance by peers or my denomination hinder my growth in worship?

_____

_____

_____

Who do my children regularly see me devote my allegiance to?

_____

_____

_____

_____

Precious in His Sight

Day nineteen

Children, especially little girls, like to know that they're pretty. Unfortunately, our society values looks over the heart. Sociological studies of the past used to try to discern if criminals had a certain "look" so that police could profile people better. The research proved invalid. God uses us unattractive or unskilled people to be instruments of righteousness or witnessing vessels so that when we succeed at a task that appears impossible or unnatural, people see Christ in us and think, "Wow! He/She did that? That *must* be God!

Did you know that Jesus was unattractive? It's true. The Bible says he wasn't much to look at (Isah. 53:2-3). If you look at artwork of Him, you usually see the stud-like Jesus. No one wants to think of worshipping an ugly Messiah, except maybe the Buddhists - the fatter the better. I never understood that. How could their god come to save the whole world and teach discipline when he couldn't even monitor his own caloric intake?! The same is true with our pictures of Adam and Eve. They both look so sexy in the artwork. Our culture loves beauty and hates imperfection, even with our cultural icons. Everyone remembers Elvis as "The King," that hot young guy rocking the mike and wooing the ladies, not the bloated, drug-induced zombie who died on the toilet.

So what do we tell our teen children if they're not the beauty queen or studly quarterback? Tough question. We don't want to highlight their flaws, but we also don't want to over-exaggerate how good-looking they are because they'll see right through it: "No, Sweetie. That's not a big mole. That's a beauty mark," or "I don't know why they call you pepperoni face with your acne, Honey. You look beautiful to me!" Rather than try to talk them *out* of their feelings, just reflect them and honor them. That's right, honor the feelings.

Sometimes we fear that if we reflect the negative feelings, we will be increasing them, but we won't. You could say, "Yeah, those comments really hurt. Kids can be cruel." You may even follow it up with a story about your own flaws, inadequacies, and experiences with rejection. The greatest studs or "studettes," either by natural beauty or that from *Extreme Makeover* plastic surgery, will all face the same laws of gravity and physics as the rest of us. It's all a matter of time.

Unfortunately, you can't pass that truth onto a teen because it doesn't line up with their emotional experience developmentally. With a gentle approach, our children can come to know that their true beauty and significance comes through Jesus Christ. Notice I said "gentle" approach rather than trying to *argue* their significance and beauty through Christ at the time.

The question we need to ask ourselves as parents is this: When a child reflects back upon our reactions to when they were sad, will they remember how we honored their feelings and listened with an open heart or that we lectured them or tried to talk them out of it - which they experience as *invalidating* and *dishonoring*? We want our children to grow up and return to us for guidance when they need it. We help determine that by the emotional climate we created *before* they left the nest.

If they think we're going to give them an "I told you so" response or unsolicited advice, they may be resistant to asking for help. We mean well, but if we are to emotionally help our children, we must first start with where they *are*. Likewise, we cannot allow our own feelings of inadequacy or our own difficulty facing tough emotions to serve as a scapegoat for not honoring our children and empathizing with their pain.

Application Exercises

How comfortable am I honoring my children's feelings without trying to rationalize or talk them out of them?

_____

_____

_____

_____

How do I feel when someone tries to cheer me up with shallow
bumper sticker therapy with messages of "Smile, God loves you,"
"Cheer up," or "Don't worry be happy"? What would I prefer
they do?

_____

_____

_____

_____

Preparing for "Game Day"

Day twenty

My daughter is trying a lot of different activities as we offer her opportunities to build mastery in fine and gross motor skills to help build self-confidence. Right now, it's soccer. When she gets older, she'll have to regularly attend the weekday practices if she is to play in the big game on Saturdays. Saturdays are the days when all that hard work and devotion pay off. Can you imagine how awkward and uncoordinated she would be if she didn't practice at *all* during the week and just showed up on Saturday? She'd probably feel out of place.

The same is true for us on Sunday mornings if we haven't regularly walked with the Lord during the week. We may feel tired, drained, and out of place. We wonder, "What do we do again? Oh, that's right. Sing this, say this, stand here, kneel there, Alleluia, and have a seat." The sacred becomes the mundane. The familiar becomes ritualistic boredom.

Sunday is a time to share our week with others in the Body of Christ, to help build up others and offer accountability and encouragement (Hebrews 10:25). Do we do that or do we slowly crawl into service via stealth mode, either after the tithe or after the part where they greet each other, only to hide and take in the sermon as we may a movie or classroom talk? "Entertain us preacher!" we sometimes think. He's not there to *entertain* us. He's there to *supplement* the spiritual disciplines we're to have *been* practicing all week.

Attending church, plugging into a ministry, and serving others is a lively, interactive adventure. Too often we think of it as a spectator sport: "Great talk Rev, see you next week. I'll keep practicing closing my eyes and resting during prayer like I did during that service," or "Wasn't that Christmas service special with all the flowers and candles? I can't wait to see the service at *Easter!*"

Just like people's exercise resolutions from New Year's die out around February, so do our emotions and commitment after a Sunday service if we don't plug into His Living Word throughout the week. Our spiritual muscles get weak and we put on weight, namely condemnation, guilt, and worry, to name a few. Jesus says that we are to yoke ourselves to Him so that our burden will be light (Matt. 11:30). We are to do this daily rather than using Sunday service as a bail-me-out plea to God (Ps. 55:22).

It's hard enough remembering names of folks in the service when we go to greet them. I never want to turn and see Jesus standing there beside me in service saying, "Good Morning, and you are...?"

Application Exercises

What do my attitude and actions Sunday morning reflect about my spiritual disciplines of the week?

_____

_____

_____

_____

What daily spiritual disciplines help me build endurance for the big game in life?

_____

_____

_____

_____

Think of a time when your regular walk with Christ during the week helped magnify your Sunday experience. What does it feel like to show up Sunday without the practice?

_____

_____

_____

_____

Day twenty-one

My daughter and I were walking to my SUV one day and she picked up a dandelion and handed it to me. It was sweet. My little girl handing her daddy a flower. Of course, it wasn't a flower to me. It was a *weed*, and it made me think of how I hadn't mowed the lawn! In a flash, I twisted a beautiful sentiment from my daughter into a personal failure message. I was blinded to the beauty of it all.

How often do we regularly blind ourselves to the beauty and awe of God's creation? While the spiders can scare us, they also serve an important purpose in killing other bugs that drive us crazy. Is a spider web an intricately spun art piece that reflects a beautiful spectrum of color in the sun, or is it annoying bug spit we quickly dismiss and swat away?

While walking my daughter to the bus one day, she pointed out the earthworms on the road from the previous day's showers. Some were dead and dried out, others were moping along. There was a whole pile of them. I got a flash in my mind of the film *Saving Private Ryan* during the first twenty minutes of the film with all that carnage. I couldn't help but think of that poor worm crawling through the bodies of his dried out comrades. Yeah, I know. I'm personifying and am being pretty imaginative in my creative license here.

63

I tell you, thought, it helped me appreciate God's creatures more, and hence God, more. Can you imagine the beat of an ant's heart? Think how small that is! That came from evolution? Umph...every creature and everything in the world has beauty to it, if you look upon it with an open heart. We need to open our eyes and experience the awesomeness of God's creation.

Application Exercises

What are some common, everyday objects in nature from God that I overlook?

_____

_____

_____

_____

Just from your house to your car and then your car to the store, walk and listen, taking in God's creations with *all* of your senses. Ask yourself, "What do I notice? List them here.

_____

_____

_____

_____

Day twenty-two

My daughter has several dolls that lie

in a praying posture and say, "Now I lay me down to sleep…" They're cute and a good start for a child in learning how to pray. Unfortunately, as parents we may continue praying in that fashion, and the Bible warns us against praying with vain repetitions (Mat. 6:7). I did the same thing with repetition growing up. Every night I said the Lord's Prayer, not really grasping its meaning. I'd sing hymns in church from memory, never paying attention to the words. During dinnertime, I really stretched myself. I had <u>two</u> prayers! "God is great. God is good. Let us thank Him for our food. Amen," and "Bless this food which now we take and make us good for Jesus' sake. Amen".

While I want to quickly get to my food and sleep just as much as the next guy, I now try to pray from my heart rather than a rote verse. I don't always *feel* like it. It's easier to take the shortcut and spit out a verse. Praying really is a *labor* of love. With my children now, I encourage them to talk to God regularly without feeling they have to approach Him with something formal. God is right there with us at the table and bedside. We don't have to make an appointment or put on fancy airs.

Too often, we may believe the house has to be clean enough for the queen of England before we invite guests over. We save the fancy silver or china from our wedding for special company…that never comes. Often times, we treat God in prayer the same way. We can have a healthy reverence for God and still enjoy the intimacy of our relationship with Him, coming to Him *just as we are*. We can pray to God as often as we want, whenever we want. The Bible instructs us to pray unceasingly (1 Thes. 5:17). He will always listen to us, whether we're in our fanciest duds or in our birthday suit! Both the quantity and quality of the prayer *is* important, but not *so* much that we become legalistic and rigid about it and end up doing nothing.

Application Exercises

Does my prayer reflect a genuine expression of my heart or an impressive display of memorization? How?

_____

_____

_____

_____

Is my relationship with Christ personal or impersonal? How?

_____

_____

_____

_____

How do I teach and model prayer to my children?

_____

_____

_____

_____

Day twenty-three

Grace Through Natural Consequences

Often times, a strong-willed child will reject our pleas for good hygiene—whether it be brushing teeth, using deodorant, or washing clothes. This is especially true during the teen years when hormones flow and new scents emerge. Then again, my son is 11 months old and has a little foot smell, but, of course, he's a baby, so it's cute...for now.

Assuming that a child does not have a genuine mental health disorder that prevents him from following through with self-care or self-awareness of the effects of hygiene on social skills, I invite parents to choose their battles. If their teen child wants to go to school with yesterday's used clothes, I say let them. This is for teens, mind you. Younger children need firmer guidance, whereas with teens, there is room to experiment Sometimes there is one thing we can't give our children: experience. Peer pressure is sometimes more valuable than parental recommendations.

If a somewhat rebellious teen wakes up and the only directions he knows (or wants to know) on how to put on his underwear is yellow in the front, brown in the back, I say go for it! *Let* his *peers* point out his funk. He or she is either going to want a girlfriend/boyfriend or a job, and poor hygiene prevents both. They'll shape up soon enough. While I do recommend honoring a teen's free will in moderation (assuming their actions aren't illegal or compromising to the spiritual integrity of the household), I also recommend they *are* instructed to clean up for dinner, church, and other family-based occasions.

It's usually our fears as parents that guide our thoughts. We think that if our child goes to school smelling funky, then all the other kids' parents will get together in a huddle and ponder, "What kind of parent would allow their child to do that?" That doesn't happen. That's *our* fear. Grace and correction are key principles here, too.

I remember an episode of "Leave It to Beaver" where Beaver refused to dress up for the dance because his friends said they'd be wearing all of these cool, casual outfits. Ward, the father, warned him otherwise but Beaver wouldn't listen. His friends were the real deal and he knew better. Of course, when Ward drove Beave to the dance in his casuals, the kids arrived at the dance all wearing suits and Beaver felt stupid. It was then the father paused, allowed the child's feelings to convict him, and only *then* did he go to the trunk and retrieve the child's hidden suit that Dad had packed earlier.

This is a valuable lesson in how to extend grace to a child, allowing them to learn in their own time but loving them and correcting with grace. Moms and Dads, keep some breath mints, wet naps, and deodorant/cologne in the glove compartment. Your kids *will* need you. They just don't know it yet.

Of course, God does the same with us. He extends free will and while we always have to experience the natural, emotional consequences of our sinful ways, He is always our loving father, waiting with open arms to embrace us and welcome us back into the fold *without* an, "I told you so."

Application Exercises

In what ways do I extend free will to my children and allow them to learn from life experience, while also loving them through it and discerning when to help and when not to?

_____

_____

_____

_____

How have I turned away from God in my life? How did He respond when I asked for forgiveness and repented for my sins?

_____

_____

_____

_____

How many times in the Bible, especially in the Old Testament where God's people regularly disobeyed, did he say, "I told you so?" Why not?

_____

_____

_____

_____

Day twenty-four

It's important that we teach our children proper manners. We usually do this by starting out with the simple ones such as saying, "thank you", "goodbye", "please", and maybe "yes, ma'am", and "no, ma'am". These beginnings and endings of conversations are an important part of instilling healthy social development.

The same is true with our relationship with God. How often do we have trouble opening up a conversation with God? Either because we've sinned and we think we can't go to Him, or, perhaps, we figure we don't know where to start. At other times, it may simply be that we don't *feel* like talking.

I'm a huge reader, and I love visiting Christian bookstores. As you can probably tell by my writings, I like to be humorous and am very child-like, so I like toy stores and gadgets as well. "Boys and their toys" you could say. When I'm feeling down, I sometimes make the mistake of walking around a bookstore or toy store looking for that "answer," or something to self-medicate with to make me "feel" good or pick me up.

What I really need is God. It is usually a wound of inadequacy or loneliness that I'm trying to numb. I usually need some reassurance that I'm doing okay. Remember the Waylon Jennings' song lyric, "Looking for love in all the wrong places, looking for love…?" That's me.

As I travel down the isles I will regularly hear God's voice or the Holy Spirit gently patting me on the shoulder saying, "Ahem. Brent…

I'm right here. It's me, God. You're not going to find me in a book. Well, maybe *one*. You want to hear from me personally, don't you? Let's talk." While my spirit is sensitive enough to discern that invitation, there were times in the past when I didn't know where to start or how to open the conversation. Then I would be reminded that *that* is indeed where to begin: "I don't know where to begin Lord. I just feel so…"

True intimacy is being naked on the *inside*. We need to allow ourselves to be transparent to God even when our feelings suggest doing just the opposite. Books, tapes, makeup, clothes, toys, food only help decorate the shields guarding our hearts more. Unfortunately, they suffocate the voice of our hearts we so desperately want our Heavenly Father to hear, while also muffling the response from Him we long to receive.

Application Exercises

What earthly rituals do I do when I am afraid of being transparent with God? What possessions do I put my faith in to comfort me instead of God?

_____

_____

_____

_____

What feelings do I usually try to self-medicate with entertainment or possessions rather than seeking restoration from God?

_____

_____

_____

What has worked for me in the past in opening a conversation with God?

_____

_____

_____

Making a Joyful Noise

Day twenty-five

If you have kids, then you too suffer from the endless brain-grating broken record of disgusting children's songs from America's best-loved dinosaur, Barney, and other annoying animals, singing, "I love you, you love me, we're a happy family, with a great big hug…" You know what I'm talking about. Admit it. You also know, "Fruit Salad…yummy, yummy" (from the Wiggles). If you don't know what I'm talking about, then get on your knees right now, and thank the good Lord for His hand of protection over your ears!

All kidding aside though, songs help uplift our children and us as well. They motivate us. They pull us out of the daily blahs of life. If we're going to get something in our head, why not gospel music? Not everyone is into Bill Gaither, Yolanda Adams or whoever is on the radio. It really doesn't matter. The key is to finding the musical style that you like, whether it be reggae, rap, heavy metal, classical, light favorites, etc., and finding it in the Christian bookstores. It's amazing what's there. The more you listen, the more it gets into your spirit because the songs usually contain scripture and the Bible is the Living Word of God. It not only aids in scripture memory but it is another tool the Holy Spirit will use when you are having a hard time.

Have you ever had the experience of nonchalantly going through your day and suddenly having a song pop into your mind? Increasing sensitivity in your spirit by spending time in the Word and in worship will help you in time of need as He gives you a pick-me-up just when you need it, either by reminding you of a song or scripture. One activity that can be helpful is to take your favorite secular song or television theme song and rewrite the words using scripture, testimony, story, whatever. Apologetix is a good band that is like a Christian Weird Al Yankovic in that they rewrite lyrics from famous contemporary songs and put them to biblical principles.

Try writing some fun lyrics to your favorite tune, even Barney's stuff. It really can be a lot of fun. Reading this suggestion, it probably sounds like a cheesy idea, but it works. And what works, works.

Application Exercises

How can I inject some creativity in my worship time and scripture memorization time?

_____

_____

_____

_____

Name a favorite tune and rewrite the lyrics to what is going on in your life or substitute the words with Scripture. Write out how it feels to write and sing. Are you willing to challenge and stretch your definition of worship? Why or why not?

_____

_____

_____

_____

Day twenty-six

My son is eating regular foods now and loves it. Prior to his growing teeth, you could really see the pain and yearning in his face as he smelled and watched the food he couldn't eat yet at the table. Unfortunately, even though he can eat it now, we still have to be sure to put down small portions of food at a time because too much on a plate confuses him and he won't eat as much. The same is true in our relationship with God.

Sometimes we want so much for God to bless us. And just as I want to give my son exciting new foods to try, God too, looks on us lovingly, but we don't have "spiritual teeth" yet. Hence, we can't handle meat, or the difficult truths of life. We may crave God's blessings, but blessings require obedience and results in increased responsibility. As the bible points out, "too much whom is given, much is required" (Luke 12:48). Many of us have religion, but not relationship. We may crave God's blessings, but with blessings come responsibility as the Bible points out "to much whom is given, much is required" (Luke 12:48).

Ever see an unfortunate person get blessed on a game show with huge prizes? You never see that same ecstatic, crying person on the show *afterwards* when they have to pay thousands of dollars in taxes they don't have. People regularly give back prizes more than you know because they can't afford it.

Bruce Wilkenson's book *The Prayer of Jabez* was a huge bestseller a couple of years ago. It was about a prayer asking God to bless us and expand our territory. That can be overwhelming at times though, when it comes to fruition. When my wife and I first went house hunting, we saw this beautiful house that exceeded our wildest dreams. It had more rooms than we had furniture. Even though we could have afforded the house, we would have been "house broke". Even more though, I remember walking through and having mixed emotions. It was such a cool house with a patio, multiple balconies, and a master bedroom with skylight and Jacuzzi tub.

At the same time, it was a little unsettling. My emotions couldn't take it all in. I'm used to being in control and I had only known a three-bedroom apartment. This "mansion" was overwhelming to me. There was just so much space. Who was going to clean it? Knowing my laziness when it comes to me helping around the house, looking at my wife confirmed that she was wondering the same thing.

Years have passed now, and today I think I could handle it. As God would have it, with kids, equity loans, mortgage, and SUV payments, we don't have the money. God still blesses me in many other ways. I'm glad God knows what's best for us even when we don't. He gives us challenges along the way to cut our teeth for the "juicy steaks" of life ahead.

The Bible speaks of mansions in Heaven (John 14:2-3). He's preparing us for ownership! What a "Land Lord"!

Application Exercises

Am I grateful for God's blessings as He deems them or do I ask for more than I can handle?

_____

_____

_____

_____

When my children were little, what were the challenges God gave me to cut my teeth on for the challenges ahead, during the teen and adult years?

_____

_____

_____

_____

Where's Your Prayer Closet?
Day twenty-seven

When we move, kids need to be a part of the process so they can manage their emotions better and feel a sense of control or mastery over their environment. This can be through decorating their room or helping to house-hunt. We all like to have a special room, place, or thing, perhaps it's a favorite chair, or a favorite place in the city you like to visit. Wherever it is, more than likely, you already know about it. Even if it's a place from a memory that helps you relax just by thinking about it. Having gone to Radford University in Radford, Virginia, the mountains and campus are so beautiful to me. Often times when I'm stressed, I'll sometimes use mental imagery and take a walk along the campus in my mind to help relax.

The Bible talks about us having a special prayer closet (Matt.6:6), someplace sacred that we may be able to talk and pray openly. When we're drained and need replenishment and hope, going to God is the best remedy.

Application Exercises

Where is my "prayer closet" or special place to talk with God?

_____

_____

_____

_____

If I don't have one, what kind of qualities would I look for in creating a "prayer closet" for myself?

_____

_____

_____

_____

Day twenty-eight

It's important as parents that we give our children choices so that they can feel some control over their world, and also to help foster decision making ability. In the battle to get dressed in the morning, we may give them two choices: "you can wear the red outfit or the blue one. Which one?" And then if they don't choose, we pick one for them. Giving them choices is important. Deciding everything for them makes them feel controlled and they rebel.

This is a normal part of a child's development during the toddler years. While giving them choices is important, too many choices or a blank check approach to parenting where they always get to pick out what they want to eat, what to wear, when to go to bed, etc., produces anxiety in a toddler because they do need guidance and direction. This blank check approach also reinforces overindulgence, leading to a spoiled child that doesn't know how to accept no for an answer and doesn't adapt well or accept life on life's terms.

Our ability to handle adversity in life is directly related to how we were taught to manage emotions and solve problems as a child. Setting limits for our children prepares them for the real world. Children need to know that manipulation and whining don't work when our "no" means "no." (Matt. 5:37).

There was a news special on television one night where the newscaster was trying to train his dog who kept biting and disobeying him. The specialist recommended that he try being firmer in his voice and demonstrate to the dog that his master was in charge. The dog really wanted the master to be in charge. It wasn't until the newscaster had gotten firm and demonstrated leadership and control that the dog could relax and not have to bite, snip, rebel, and disobey commands.

The same is true for children. While they say they want to do everything they want when they want to, children not only require structure and guidance, they secretly *want* it even if they don't know how to request it. They're not supposed to. We're the parents.

Here's an example of what you will *not* hear in a household from a toddler: "You know, Mom, you really should be consistent with my meal times and my bed-times. That way, my biological clock will respond to the consistency and my emotions won't be so fluctuating. Plus, all this fast food, sugar, and caffeine are messing with my moods and attitude. I need a well-balanced diet so that I can perform well at school and behave."

It is our job as parents to be leaders in our households. That means educating ourselves in healthy parenting skills so that our children will comply and come under our direction and authority. This is even more necessary for strong-willed children as outlined in Dr. James Dobson's book, *The Strong-Willed Child*.

God gives us free will, and yet when it comes to the basic truth to either follow Him or not, there are two choices: obey or disobey. Children don't realize it, but their lives would go so much easier for them if they would just do what we told them. We're experienced and when we recommend something, we're doing it out of love with their best interests in mind. The same is true with God and us. He expects us to lead a righteous life, while still obeying and coming under *His* authority.

When my wife and I are not holding hands in public, I catch myself walking in malls and parking lots several feet in front of her. I'm the scout. It's an inborn characteristic of the hunter versus gatherer. It's an I-go-forward-and-see-if-it's-safe kind of thing. I'm the spiritual head of the household. I'm the leader, the protector. God is *our* protector. He leads. He scouts. Do we *allow* Him to? Do we trust in His sovereign will that *He* knows what is best for us and that He makes everything work out for His good and His divine purposes? (Romans 8:28).

Application Exercises

How do I demonstrate humility to follow God's truths and

recommendations even when my emotions challenge me to do things *my* way?

_____

_____

_____

_____

How do I demonstrate and model a Christ-like leadership to my spouse and children?

_____

_____

_____

_____

Carrying the Torch
Day twenty-nine

God says that we are the light of the world and we are to be the salt of the earth (Matt. 5:13). Salt has many uses. One, it's a preservative. We are to keep Jesus' original message of love and salvation and carry it to the people. Two, salt heals a wound. I can remember as a little boy, when I had a cut, my family used to have this medication salt stick. It hurt like the dickens but it stopped the bleeding when applied to cuts.

Sometimes, as Christians, our message stings those who don't want to hear the truth. As parents, we have an important duty to pass on an emotional and spiritual legacy, keeping alive Jesus' message, but also preventing against intergenerational curses to our descendants. Just like when the Holy Spirit convicts us of our wrong doings and God disciplines us with his rod and staff, it can hurt sometimes as we ponder having to face the consequences of our sinful actions.

Application Exercises

What will my child's spouse learn about them and how they were raised?

_____

_____

_____

_____

What will my parenting reflect?

_____

_____

_____

_____

What will future generations say about me and the life I led?

_____

_____

_____

_____

What is the spiritual legacy I want to pass on to my descendants?

_____

_____

_____

_____

Day thirty

Every week, my daughter and I have a tea party. She really looks forward to it. It's just one of our many sacred father-daughter rituals. She thinks it's about fun and spending time with Daddy. Although that's part of it, there's more going on. As a father, I am responsible for teaching my daughter how she should be treated as a woman. I'm also role modeling whom to date. This involves living out a Christ-like life for her to relate to.

She regularly sees how I treat my wife with affection, cooperation, and loyalty. She also sees arguments and the resolution process. She sees how our relationship commitment, friendship and most importantly, our relationship with Christ help us sustain any emotional, physical, or spiritual pressures we face. She sees us praying and practicing servanthood.

Creating this lifestyle for ourselves and obeying God not only enriches our lives, but ensures that my children know what mental, spiritual and emotional health looks like. It's like planting seeds. If I plant hate, bitterness, unforgiveness, disorganization, and chaos, I will see it in my children. They will associate these traits with love and thus seek out relationships in life that are similar.

Likewise, my son is being raised to be Christ-like. He learns manners, chivalry, honor, and respect. He sees me love my wife like Christ loves the church (Eph. 5:25).

It is important as parents that we never underestimate the importance of quality time with our children. Children learn who they are and how to manage emotions in their relationship with us. Who they are and the role they play in the family will either give them security and purpose to go out into the world and seek God's will, or they will go to the world *for* that identity and emotional security. Unfortunately, this takes on the form of sex, drugs, alcohol, gangs, etc. Our families are like beehives. If we don't want our kids to fly away and seek acceptance and validation elsewhere through corrupt relationships and/or destructive behaviors, then we need to create more "honey" at home.

Family rituals, traditions, game nights, theme nights, mealtimes, devotional times, and even tea parties help solidify us as a family unit and give our children a clear picture of healthy relationships and fellowship.

What we do with our toddlers now can prevent major problems during the teen and adult years. At the same time, through Christ, parent-child relationships can be nurtured and improved at *any* age. Satan would love nothing more than for us as parents to give up and think that we can't have an impact in our children's lives, and that it's too late. The world, the media, and the enemy are always willing to imprint their values onto our children.

Reality is that the older our children get, the more they will need to make decisions for themselves. It is our job to provide them with the correct resources. Remember that we are to "train a child up in the way he should go, and when he is old he will not turn from it" (Prov. 22:6).

Application Exercises

List the important rituals, traditions, and family fun nights at your house.

_____

_____

_____

_____

If you don't have any family traditions, create a list here. Your children may dislike family activities or think it's "uncool" if you haven't modeled this in a while. They may lack healthy attachment skills. If you hold these bonding opportunities sacred and stay consistent, they *will* want to be a part of this nurturing.

_____

_____

_____

_____

What are some of my character traits that I want to instill in my children?

_____

_____

_____

_____

What are some of my character traits I don't want to instill in my children? Am I willing to give up my vices and my ways to be a role model for my children? Why or why not?

_____

_____

_____

_____

What are the traits and traditions of my parents that I want to include and exclude in my relationship with my children?

_____

_____

_____

_____

Exposure to the Son

Day thirty-one

My children love to laugh and I like to laugh with them. Have you ever noticed that when you read to your children, if you make it humorous, they want to hear that same story over and over again? I've always been intrigued how some adults could read a favorite novel over and over again. A lot of times as parents, we may get bored rereading a children's book, but research shows that repetitive reading to children still enhances brain functioning and literacy skills.

The same is true for us reading the Bible. Sometimes it's natural; sometimes it's "fake and bake." This is how we hear from God. As the Bible says in Romans 10:17, "So faith comes from hearing, and hearing by the word of God." The Bible teaches us that its contents are literally God's word. God's breath. His *Living Word* written by men as God divinely inspired and wrote through them. His word and truth work through our lives much like getting a suntan. The more you get the sun and/or Son (Jesus) in you, the darker you get. The more you are away from it, the paler you get.

People like to compliment others on their tan. Sometimes, it's natural, sometimes, it's "fake and bake" from a tanning salon. The same is true in our reading of scripture. We can tan naturally by engaging in daily spiritual disciplines that help us embrace the word of God or we can try to fake it at church and *appear* spiritual. Our children are watching us and God is too.

What are we teaching to others? We may be the only opportunity our children, neighbors, and strangers in the community have to see God. Let's be a witness to others, especially our children. Our children may forget when they get older which book they read the most with us, but they'll never forget the time we spent with them and how special we made them feel during that time.

Application Exercises

How have I helped model the importance of God's word in my children's lives?

_____

_____

_____

_____

Do my children understand the value the Bible has not only for them, but also for me?

_____

_____

_____

_____

Day thirty-two

Children have a natural curiosity about the world around them. They love to ask us "why" questions a lot. Sometimes it appears that no answer will satisfy them. It's an endless quest to find truth and understanding. The same is true for us. We have a lot of "why" questions for God, especially during troubling experiences.

Some of us were raised never to question God. That's just not biblical. God wants us to have an open and honest relationship with Him. We can come to him with our "whys" and even our anger. Check out the Psalms.

David questions God's whereabouts in Psalm 22:1. Even Christ asks the similar question on the cross, "My God, My God, why have You forsaken Me?" (Mark 15:34). He knew that He came to die for us and yet He *still* asked God that! When He allowed the sin of the world to enter Him, He lost His knowledge of God (and His everlasting love), just like Adam and Eve did in the Garden when they sinned. I'm glad Jesus asked that question, because it tells me if the Son of God, who has all the answers of the universe, can have questions and doubts, so can I. And so can we.

When we get tired of answering our children's endless barrage of questioning, we sometimes try to put on a good face that it doesn't bother us. We want to be encouraging to them so they will seek us out. Likewise, we may think that God is too busy for us. That is untrue and un-biblical. I'm glad God never tires of our questions!

No matter how many questions our children ask, how we answer demonstrates whether they can trust us or not with their questions. I never want my children to be afraid to seek me out for answers. This includes when it requires me to humbly respond with, "That's a great question. I don't know." The same is true for us, as our Heavenly Father reminds us to be, "anxious for nothing but in everything, by prayer and petition, with thanksgiving, make your requests known to God." (Phil. 4:6).

Application Exercises

Am I candid with my questions to God? Why or why not?

_____

_____

_____

_____

Do I model grace and understanding like Christ does with us when my children ask "Why?" questions?

_____

_____

_____

_____

As parents, it is important that we teach our children how to help themselves along the way rather than depend on us solely because we may not always be there. It's important that we show them the resources for answers. This may be a Bible passage on how to deal with one of life's problems or it could be a dictionary or thesaurus to help them write a paper. It's okay to help children but not to do *all* the work for them. We need to teach our children resourcefulness, creativity, a desire to learn, to grow and to explore. Even Jesus spoke to his disciples in parables or puzzles to stimulate their thinking rather than just giving them the answers straight out. He wants the same for us.

The Bible is written for everyone of every socioeconomic background, race, and gender. We are often suckered into believing that the scriptures are too foreign for us or that we need the theologians to help break it down for us simpletons. Bookstores often sell books with catchy titles about Bible "secrets". I can remember buying a video touting it had the secret way Jesus taught His disciples to pray!

The Bible is clear on this. Not only does the Bible assure us that there is nothing new (Ecc. 1:9), Matthew 6 discusses Jesus' specific directions how to pray when they asked Him to teach them. There is no secret knowledge. The Bible is God's gift to us and it is open to everyone! God never intended for His Living Word to be treated as a secret for only a select few or a specially chosen group. That's where all the other religions are lost and deceived in their desire to add "lost scriptures" to the Bible.

God also never meant for His Living Word to be carelessly read like a novel. We are to study it. There are many resources for us to use to help understand the Bible, including concordances, Bible dictionaries, commentaries, and Bible studies. Do we role model using resources to study the scriptures to our children or do we just show up Sunday morning seeking out the preacher to give us the Cliff Notes version?

While it is nice to enjoy a meal out at a fancy restaurant, have you ever noticed how much more fulfilling it is to *make* a dinner? To be involved with the process? There is a much greater appreciation for the process when we're an active participant. The same is true for researching the Bible. Studying the Bible ourselves gives us a richer understanding and leads to a more intimate relationship with God.

There are many great teachers out there and many books, tapes, and DVDs. I encourage you to look at these as *supplements* to your *own* study. Just as our children's teachers want to give them a true learning experience rather than having them just gobble up the latest Cliff notes or catching the book on film, so does Christ call us into a personal relationship with Him if we will seek Him out. It's about relationship, not religion.

Application Exercises

Do I seek the Bible out and explore it, and study it the way God intended, or do I allow others to do it for me? Why or why not?

_____

_____

_____

_____

What lies have I bought into that have prevented me from believing that I can study the Bible the way God intended?

_____

_____

_____

_____

Comfort During the Storm

Day thirty-four

I can remember as a child when my father took me out to ride a bike. Even though I felt secure with my father holding the seat and running beside me, it was both thrilling and scary because I didn't actually know at times when he would let go. When the big day came for them to be removed, he took me out and held the back of my seat as I rode. Eventually, he would let go and I'd ride by myself. The first time I fell he would *pick* me up. The second time I fell, he'd *help* me up. I would keep riding and the third time I fell, he'd allow me to get up *by myself*. While I would get injured at times, he'd love me *through* it, and my endurance and resolution to master the bike would crystallize. I was going to do it! I can remember singing the theme from the movie *Rocky* as I pedaled down the street.

As a parent, that childhood experience with my father takes on a whole new meaning. While it was both thrilling and scary for me because I felt secure with my father holding the seat and running beside me, I didn't actually know at times when he let go. That must have been hard on *him* too. Would he blame himself when I fell? It couldn't have been a great feeling to see me fall down and get banged up. And yet it was a natural part of childhood that my father endured *with* me. He never enabled me or told me anything was too tough. He let me work hard. Today, I too foster the inner daredevil in my kids. Whether it be them jumping off the edge of the pool into my arms or my tossing up of my toddler in the air, their confidence and trust in our relationship grows.

The same is true with our relationship with God. Faith is an action word. He allows difficult times to strengthen our faith and draw us into a more loving, intimate walk with Him. Just as my father loved me through the cuts and bruises, so does God. He doesn't relish in our failures and flops. He loves us *through* them. That's an important revelation especially when everyone asks, "Why does God let bad things happen to good people?"

While theological answers will not minister to the emotional distress we will encounter during our personal crises, it is helpful to ground ourselves to the reality of God's character as written in the Bible and also how His faithfulness helped us weather storms from the past.

Application Exercises

How has God sustained me through problems in the past?

_____

_____

_____

_____

Did my previous complaints and doubts about God during those times pan out?

_____

_____

_____

_____

In what ways do our children trusting in us parallel our walk with God?

_____

_____

_____

_____

Day thirty-five

Earlier I mentioned how God does not delight in having to discipline us. Neither do I when my children act out. Yet the decision to discipline children is not whether it *feels* good but if it's necessary, and it is. Growing up, I never understood the old cliché of "this will hurt you more than it hurts me." As a parent though, I recognize its truth. Spanking, restricting privileges, enforcing timeouts, etc. are all draining and affect the family as a whole. Flexibility is necessary as events may become postponed and expectations challenged.

God disciplines us when we sin and try to follow our own will rather than His. Likewise, it would be irresponsible and bad parenting if we did not discipline our children in *some* way to set boundaries and limits. Proverbs 3:11-12 states, "My son, do not despise the chastening of the Lord, nor detest His correction; For whom the Lord loves He corrects. Just as a father the son *in whom* he delights."

Without limits and boundaries for us, anxiety ensues because we don't know where we stand and what we can do. Like a lamb astray, God's rod and staff comfort [us] (Psalm 23:4). The same is true for us as parents. We can offer our children emotional security, guiding them in the right path and allowing them to trust us when they know no better. This, of course, entails a greater level of accountability in our lives as we humble ourselves and yoke ourselves to Christ for His correction of *us*.

One day I was driving by a neighborhood college billboard. It said, "Follow the grain in your own wood." I remember thinking what a cool saying that was and then the Holy Spirit quickened me, stating that it was a good saying, as long as the wood was that of the *cross*. We all have free will, but if we "trust in the Lord with all of [our] heart and lean not on [our] own understanding" (Proverbs 3:5-6), we'll truly live a more fulfilling life.

Just like Moses spent 40 years in the desert when it could have taken 11 days if he had followed directions, we may take a more arduous detour in our life the longer we defy God. This is similar to my children deciding how long they'll cause a strain in our relationship. Eventually though, as children, they will bend to our will, whether it be eating vegetables or going to school. The same is true for us with God as one day, "at the name of Jesus every knee should bow, in heaven and on earth and under the earth, and every tongue confess that Jesus Christ is Lord, to the glory of God the Father." (Phil. 2:10).

While our children are still children, we know what's best for them, but God knows what is best for us our *entire life*!

Application Exercises

How has God disciplined me in my sin?

_____

_____

_____

_____

How long have I or had I postponed following God's will for my life? What were the consequences?

_____

_____

_____

_____

Day thirty-six

To some extent we all rebel. We do this to our parents, bosses, and spouses. Whether it be actions such as cursing, breaking rules, overspending, overeating, or drinking too much, we all want to do things our way. Children are no different. My daughter is in her "let me do it" mode and she likes to prove to my wife and I how much she can do for herself. As children grow up, they seek more and more to establish their uniqueness, their identity, and their place in this world. As parents, this can sometimes be unsettling as we work to help them establish balance between maintaining the family values and norms with their own opinions and personalities. These don't have to be mutually exclusive.

Children want to explore the world with all its colors, clothes, and hairstyles, all to our chagrin. While we don't want to foster a rebellious spirit towards God and our family values, keep in mind that children often establish their uniqueness in being different from us, and they like to try to challenge us in this. Nurturing their creativity in this process can be helpful.

I remember overhearing a child with a friend one day in my office's waiting room. They had decided to switch shoes and surprise Mom. When she came out to see them, her son exclaimed, "Look, Mom, we're wearing each others' shoes!" This child was just having fun and looking for a little shock value. The mother ordered the son to switch shoes back and the child played it off, shrugging, "Okay, Mom."

A better alternative might have been to feign disgust saying, "Ooh. Stinky!" at which point the two kids would have laughed and felt a playful sense of power at their little rebellion. Offering safe little rebellions like this prevent a child from feeling over-controlled. Too often we as parents may be controlling and have rigid expectations to which a child may want to break free from the family system and explore unhealthy experiences such as drugs, alcohol, and sex.

Do we get to know our children and their hobbies, desires, goals, and dreams, or do we focus on making them just like us? Do we confuse rebellion with personal style?

Children who don't have good communication skills will often express themselves through their dress or music. Wearing black or listening to weird music doesn't have to be about Satan or an evil influence. Many times children just want to fit in or they like a music group for their ability to do what they can't, which is to express themselves and have a point of view.

As parents we owe it to ourselves and our children to sit down and have open discussions about our identity and theirs, as well as their likes and dislikes. What message are they really trying to convey? Do the children really understand the lyrics that they're singing, or are they just listening to the beat? Does wearing black mean Gothic and suicide, or is it just about wanting to be different and setting themselves apart?

Keep in mind that I am not endorsing anti-social behavior. I'm merely inviting you to invest in your children and get to know them. It's important not to immediately jump to conclusions and make judgments about what our children's values are. Even Sigmund Freud, who was famous for dream analysis and believing everything related to sex somehow, said, "Sometimes a cigar is just a cigar."

Application Exercises

What is unique about my child(ren)?

_____

_____

_____

_____

What are some behaviors I engaged in as a child that set me apart? How did my parents interpret them?

_____

_____

_____

_____

How have I invested in my children's hobbies and interests to validate who they are as people?

_____

_____

_____

_____

How do I know how to discern rebellion from personal style?

_____

_____

_____

_____

Being Good Enough
Day thirty-seven

Isn't it a good feeling to know that you're the right size to get on the rides at an amusement park? It's sad to have to experience that rejection with our kids when they're just short of the mark. It seems like the world always wants to size us up.

I remember growing up during Thanksgiving when there were always two tables: the adult table and the "kiddie" table. My favorite uncle was at the big table and he was always cutting up. I wanted to be there so bad.

Professionally too, it seems we need this degree or that credential, or some other worldly measure to demonstrate that we have what it takes to be significant in this world. It's frustrating and at times, downright discouraging.

I remember growing up in the church where the hymnal during communion stated, "we are not so worthy as to gather up the crumbs from under thy table." That statement didn't bother me so much until I got saved and then when I was justified through Christ's gift at the cross, God said, "Brent, come on up and eat with me!" He invites us to eat *with* Him.

It is true that only through Christ are we worthy, but at the same time, He doesn't want us to grovel. We *do need* to humble ourselves before the Lord and demonstrate a healthy reverence, but we aren't to cower at the throne. As a matter of fact, Christ invites us to approach Him with boldness (see Heb. 4:16).

Likewise, it is important that as mothers and fathers we extend the same grace to our children, letting them know that they *are* good enough. They need to know that we love them unconditionally, and that they may approach us boldly (not arrogantly but with confidence, knowing that they will be readily accepted). They need to know that while we may not agree with their choices, and we may not like their behavior, we will always love them.

I never want my children to have to think they have to legalistically live up to my expectations to be good enough. I don't want them to experience rejection with me like they do at the amusement park. Whether they are as tall as a Smurf or Flintstone is not the standard that counts in life.

Just as a branch is grafted into the vine and we are a part of the Body of Christ, so should our children feel like they are an extension of us. Not that they live in our shadow, but that we empower them to realize they are loved, not for their works, but because they're ours.

Application Exercises

To what standards do I hold my children up to?

_____

_____

_____

_____

Am I realistic in my expectations and standards with my children? Are my expectations age-appropriate?

_____

_____

_____

_____

Do I model grace in my expectations for my children as Christ does for me?

_____

_____

_____

_____

Living Up to a Name

Day thirty-eight

On the playground you can sometimes hear the chant, "Sticks and stones may break my bones but words will never hurt me." That is just one of the age-old lies we were taught as children. The fact is words do hurt and even scar. Name-calling can knock a child down and crush a spirit.

I remember reading Dale Carnegie's book, *How to Win Friends and Influence People* as a teenager and how it said that the most important word to a person is their own name.

There are many books on the market for baby names. A favorite pastime for couples is to ponder the names for their unborn child. Extensive research is done on the meanings. This was an extremely important rite of passage in the Bible too. Your name told everyone who you were. Today we think of a person's name in a more casual sense, like putting on our stamp of approval if we sign our name to it. It is part of our credibility and statement of faith, for instance when we sign a check or an I.O.U. However, in biblical times your name's *literal* meaning carried much weight.

My daughter gets a kick out of poking fun at my wife and I when she hears us use pet names such as "sweetheart" and "honey". However, she loves the entire gamut of words we use with her: "princess," "kitten," "angel," "peanut," "darling," etc.

These terms of endearment are an important part of nurturing relationships. They convey the same love that God expressed when He said of His son Jesus, "You are my Son, whom I love; with you I am well pleased." (Luke 3:22).

God's grace is sufficient when it comes to forgiveness and yet here on earth, with how we treat each other, bad names come at quite an emotional cost. It takes an awful lot of "atta boys" to override a shameful label.

Our children have a unique way of holding us accountable. Simple phrases like "shut-up" or "that sucks" seem insignificant when *we* say it. Yet, hearing it from our children we are brought into a new awareness of how distasteful those words sound.

How we treat each other is a direct reflection of how we feel about ourselves. And how we feel about ourselves is largely based on how our parents first saw us. We saw ourselves reflected through their words, and their actions. Behind every bully is a scared, insecure child who desperately wants to know that they are loved. Our children are listening to us and how we not only treat them, but others as well. What are we imprinting upon their hearts about who they are as individuals?

Application Exercises

When my child(ren) reflect back on how I treated them and others, what will they say they learned about themselves as people and their self-worth?

_____

_____

_____

_____

What were the pet names and/or labels, good or bad, my parents had for me and each other? How did that make me feel?

_____

_____

_____

_____

What terms of endearment do I use with my spouse and children?

_____

_____

_____

_____

If I could go back in time, what words would I most like to have heard from my parents?

_____

_____

_____

_____

God's Faithfulness

Day thirty-nine

Being a child is difficult. Children live in an adult world and other people are always making decisions for them - decisions that they don't understand. Challenging authority doesn't help them. It didn't work with us either.

Remember when you didn't understand something from your folks? What was their usual response? Why is it we had to do what they said? "Because I said so, that's why." "Because mother/father knows best," "You don't need to know why. Just do it." Those answers just never seemed to satisfy. Nope. It wasn't until we became parents and first heard our children's defiance did we come to realize what a silly question it was. "Who are they to question us?" we wonder as parents. "Don't they know we know best? Don't they realize the experience we have?" Nope. Neither did we when we were their age.

God has the same experience with us. The Ten Commandments are just that. Commandments. They are not the ten *suggestions*. Life doesn't seem fair at times and we wonder: "why Lord, why?" Could it be that God knows more than we do? Could it be true that he really *does* work out everything to glorify Him (Rom. 8:38)? "Naaah," we think during our trials and tribulations.

Our human minds have such trouble wrapping around tragedy. There seems to be so much injustice in the world. Especially when it happens to us. When we submit ourselves to God, He may call us to take on a certain task in fulfilling His will for our lives. Sometimes the task appears too great, or we're unwilling to do it out of personal feelings of inadequacy. The Bible is filled with stories of His people challenging His authority, and Him asking them to do tasks that didn't seem to make sense at the time.

All of the leaders in the Bible would question Him or think that He couldn't possibly be thinking that *they* were up to the task. They were so unprepared, unskilled. It's true that His ways are not our ways (Isaiah 55:8-9). That's why God uses imperfect vessels like us, so when His good works are done through us, people say, "You did what? You? That's *GOT* to be God." We are not that different from the people in the Bible.

When I first heard my daughter question my authority I thought, "Doesn't she know how much I love her? Doesn't she know the great plans I have for us as a family? I'm giving her directions to complete something so that we can have fun! Doesn't she trust that I know best? Doesn't she know how old I am? Who is she to question me? I was on this earth long before her. The fun times and ideas I have for us as a family were thought up by my wife and I long before she was born! Doesn't she know that I was the guy in the delivery room who praised God when she came into the world? Again, who is she to question me?"

Of course this was not verbalized to her. I just wondered it. And then I remember God reminding me of the passage in the Bible when He talked with Job. This is from Chapter 38 of the Message Bible: "Where were you when I created the earth? Tell me, since you know so much! Who decided on its size? Certainly you'll know that! Who came up with the blueprints and measurements? How was its foundation poured, and who set the cornerstone?" If you go back and read chapter 38 of any translation, it's a very humbling experience, especially when we are tempted to question God.

Application Exercises

How has God been faithful in meeting my needs?

_____

_____

_____

_____

How have I taught my children that God can be trusted? Have I
modeled that by fully putting my faith in Him?

_____

_____

_____

_____

How have I demonstrated trust and faithfulness to my children?

_____

_____

_____

_____

Enjoy the Ride

Day forty

Children have a unique way of

being able to enjoy the world and play. Before we and the world educate them about the limits and rules in the game of life, they can find such enjoyment in what appear to be insignificant, silly things. And that's what's beautiful about them. They're pure, untainted.

I remember my high school Chemistry teacher telling me how he had seen experts in his field have rigid ideas about equations that just couldn't be solved, and he would simply give it to students who didn't know there was no answer, and they would solve it!

Children can bring such a fresh perspective to our lives. They are gut-wrenchingly honest at times. In today's world of political correctness and euphemisms to rewrite new ways of accepting simple truths, we can learn a lot from children. God commands us to come to Him with the heart of a child. We don't need to come under false pretenses or a mask. He knows us (Psalm 139:1). He *should*. He *created* us.

Children know how to have fun and enjoy the ride. Eventually, it becomes about blue ribbons and medals, but at first, it's simply for the enjoyment, not just the end result, but also the *process*.

When we die, those of us who are saved through Christ will indeed be absent from the body and present with the Lord (2 Cor. 5:6-8). All of this will occur in the blink of an eye. While it's important to cross the finish line, Christ died so that we may have life and live it abundantly (see John 10:10) here on *earth*! His Kingdom shall be done here on earth as it is in heaven (Matt. 6:10). It can be done right *here*. We don't have to wait for some pie in the sky that we'll get to *someday!*

While you are on your fortieth devotion and have *finished* the book, have you enjoyed the *ride*? Is *completing* it more satisfying then the walk-through? Often times we ponder, who will our children become? What will their professions be? What will our grandchildren look like?

We need to be sure that we *enjoy* our children on a *daily* basis. To enjoy your children and enjoy your spouse is *not* an oxymoron! We are all a combination of strengths and weaknesses. And we are precious in His sight (Ps. 116:15). Shouldn't our children be too?

I love the scene in the movie, *Parenthood*, when Steve Martin's character is devastated at watching his kids run around the stage at the school play. They start off well, but then wreck havoc. As the camera focuses on Steve Martin's face between the ups and downs of the play, the film is dubbed over with the sound of a roller coaster with *its* many ups and downs. It's a very touching, thoughtful scene.

We are all going to experience trials and tribulations. Those are opportunities for us to draw closer to Him. It doesn't always *feel* good, but God never promised that it would. He just promised to love us *through* it (John 6:33), to give us the strength, character, and courage to persevere. Not in our own flesh (and through our *own* efforts), but through Him. Not because of what *we* can do, but what He already *did* on the cross. So, too, are we called to love our children through the good times and the bad. While He did say He would make the way of escape with regards to temptation (in a way *He* sees fit), God also promises He'll give us what we need to *bear* it" (1 Cor. 10:13). Notice how the Bible says, "Ye though [we] walk *through* the valley of the shadow of death, [we] will fear no evil…(Psalm 23:4)" It's "*through*," not "around" or "under" or "over". *Through.*

Application Exercises

How am I at accepting both my child's strengths *and* limitations?

_____

_____

_____

_____

How do I model humility in accepting weakness as a strength?

_____

_____

_____

_____

How do I demonstrate to my children a love for life as a journey rather than a destination?

_____

_____

_____

_____

The Next Step

Discover 50 in depth secrets for a Nurturing Parent-Child Relationship and Heavenly Parenting through our Bonus Interactive Exercises. To receive these free exercises, go to www.HeavenlyParenting.com and follow the directions there to your **FREE 50 SECRETS**.

Printed in the USA
CPSIA information can be obtained
at www.ICGtesting.com
JSHW082220140824
68134JS00015B/646

9 781933 596464